Doggie Devotional
God's Truths Revealed Through My Dogs
Christine Benet

Images of Madison in the "Loyalty" chapter are courtesy of Shayla Sullivan.

Cover photo and design by Susan Watson. https://www.susanwatsonphotos.com

Copy edits by K. L. Byles. https://linkedin.com/in/kimbylescopywriter

Published by A Couple of Writers. https://www.facebook.com/aCoupleOfWriters

Contents

Thank you, Kim Burdick, for the gentle challenge that got the ball rolling on this project which had been sitting somewhere in my head collecting dust. And Kim, ahem, still waiting on your book, my friend!

Thank you to my neighbor Susan for the cover photo and design, for being a first reader, for praying for this as well as providing ongoing support and encouragement.

Thank you, Wiebke, for the occasional nagging, I mean, encouragement, to get this done.

Thank you to Elaine for all the encouragement, advice, tips, and prayers.

Thank you to all who read early drafts and provided critiques.

Special thanks to Dianne, my ever present and constant cheerleader who sees only the good and possible in people and projects—and is one of Cody's favorite pet sitters.

Thank you to Joe, my steady sounding board and supporter who put countless hours into editing, critiquing, formatting, and helping me push through when I got stuck—you know you are the best!!

(This ellipsis in parenthesis is for you ...)

And ... thank you to a loving Father God who teaches me in a way my simple mind can understand and the dogs through whom He speaks.

Introduction

Aslan and my dad

The minute I hear 'doggie devotional,' I think of my dad who was born in 1926 and felt dogs were work animals who should be kept outside. He was disgusted by American culture that tends to humanize dogs and treat them as equals. I understand his viewpoint and perspective based on when and how he grew up. If it seems like I am apologizing at times in these stories due to the emphasis on dogs, I'm sure it is because I am reacting to his voice in my head.

But here's the deal. God talks to us all in a variety of ways. I believe He'll use whatever is in our environment to speak to us and teach us if we let Him. I don't have kids. I love all the cute and yet spiritually convicting stories my friends tell about their kids, but again, I don't have children. So, He sometimes uses my dogs to teach me things, and I feel there is no reason to apologize for that. When you hear the apologetic tone in my writing, please realize I'm talking to my dad, roll your eyes, and move on.

In telling these stories, I'm not elevating dogs to something equal with humans. By the way, they are WAY better at unconditional love, just sayin'. When I describe my dog's actions and compare them to our actions, I understand they are not the same. My dogs act instinctively. They may have feelings, but their critical thinking and reasoning skills are far from an adult human level. I totally get that. *Really*, I do!

Still, God has used my dogs to teach me, and I felt led to share the stories. My hope is you find them encouraging, maybe funny, maybe challenging. Perhaps He will whisper something to you through them as well. God also speaks to me through other daily experiences involving gardening, working out, nature, other people, work situations, and chance encounters. If you want to hear some of those stories, invite me out to coffee or tell me to write devotional #2.

So, there it is. (I love you, Dad.)

Enjoy!

We should all pause at times to reflect on God's truths.

Photo by Susan Watson.

1
"Let Go of the Bone!"

But seek first his kingdom and his righteousness, and all these things will be given to you as well.
MATTHEW 6:33 NIV

Harvey and his precious bone

I t was quite amusing to watch. We returned from eating our favorite pizza with scraps of crust to give our dog, Harvey, as a treat. He loved pizza crust. However, he also loved his big, fluffy, stuffed bone—so much so that as he approached his bowl containing the pizza scraps, he found himself in a predicament. He wanted the new treat, but he was not willing to let go of the bone to get it.

He stuck his head in and out of his bowl, attempting to eat the pizza crust while *also* having a mouthful of his precious, stuffed bone. His head bobbed up and down a few times. You could see his little mind spinning, trying to solve the dilemma.

He looked up at us for help and whined.

We told him to "drop it."

He whined and tried again.

He started pacing, still whining, looking at us for help. We continued telling him to "drop it" while laughing a bit at his distress. He decided to *hold* it instead and returned to the bowl to try again.

After repeating this cycle a few times, long enough for us to grab a camera and take a video, Harvey finally, hesitantly, dropped his bone and enjoyed his treat. Harvey liked his stuffed bone because, well, I don't know why. I think because it squeaked, he knew it was his, and he could lay his head on it. But it wasn't *really* a bone. It was an imitation of something—a real treat which he could actually taste, which he could eat, which would provide nourishment. Way better than a stuffed bone.

All that was cute, funny, and also kind of sad—no one threatened to take that bone away from Harvey. He could have both. The thought came to me that I do that, too. What? Who, me? No. But yes!

Am I not clinging to the imitation, stuffed bone when I am content with a full calendar thinking being busy will satisfy my need for belonging and significance? Instead, I could have the truly satisfying experience of trusting He has already said I am enough and letting Him fill my need for love and acceptance His way.

To be honest I think there are areas of my life where my refusal to let go of certain habits or beliefs blocks my ability to receive something better from God. Like I must believe, maybe even subconsciously, that this fear and anxiety thought pattern I have sometimes really works for me or I wouldn't keep choosing it, but *Lord, I want to live in Your peace.* Or I feel important and loved when I'm constantly busy, but *Lord, if You could just give me Your rest.* When I hold on to something tightly, I don't have open hands to receive from Him.

What about you? Are there places you are unwilling to surrender? Are you holding on to the fake food, blocking God from giving you real sustenance that would truly satisfy you?

I invite you to take a minute to quiet yourself and ask Him to show you any areas He would like you to let go of, or hold more loosely, so you are able to receive other, better gifts He has for you. If you hear something, you might keep going and ask what He wants to give you instead. Don't worry if you don't hear anything the first time you try this, keep asking.

2

Love Anyway

My husband, Joe, and Cody

*For he chose us in him before the
creation of the world to be holy
and blameless in his sight. In love
he predestined us for adoption to
sonship through Jesus Christ, in
accordance with his pleasure and
will—to the praise of his glorious
grace, which he has freely given us
in the One he loves.*
EPHESIANS 1:4-6 NIV

As I read the verse above for a Bible study, I started thinking about how *before* He created this world, God knew the entire story and how it would unfold. That meant He knew the lovely things man would do, but also the unspeakable, evil, depraved things man would do as well. He knew mankind would fall, and He would have to send His son Jesus to come and die a horrific death as a sacrifice for us, to bring us back into relationship with Him. Despite the significant cost, He *still* chose to set the story in motion, to love us even though we would break His heart. He chose to *love anyway*.

My thoughts drifted to the idea that as Christians, we are called to do this also—to love others even when they hurt or reject us—and wow, how poorly we live this out. Several people came to mind who, because of their unhealed places, dropped friends or built mammoth, protective walls at the slightest hurt or hint of rejection. I get it. I can be sensitive and have my feelings hurt easily and my tendency is to withdraw or avoid the person in the future. Without God's reminders to forgive offenses and keep pressing in, I would ghost many people. I thought of all the church division and infighting I've heard about over the years. We as the church should be better about this. What's that song we sing? "They'll know we are Christians by our love ..."

And then I heard God whisper gently to my spirit, "And what about Cody?"

Ouch!

We were in the process of choosing our third dog. My husband wanted another big breed. Our first pet was a 195-pound Old English Mastiff, and he was great, but I still cleaned "slingers," meaning slobber, off the walls a year after he passed.

Our second dog, Harvey, whom you met in the first story, was a fifty-five-pound, *perfect*, *adorable* Heinz 57 mutt that was easy to care for. Do I sound biased? Maybe. I would have cloned that dog. As the primary housekeeper, I was not looking forward to a dog that shed or had BIG, DIRTY paws, and was angling toward a hypoallergenic, non-shedding, eighty-pound doodle of some sort as a compromise.

We were including Anatolian Shepherds in our search and a local Great Dane rescue had an Anatolian/Great Dane mix available—as the DNA test revealed though, Cody is actually 50% Great Dane and 50% Great Pyrenes. The first adoption had not gone well, and he had been returned. The foster family indicated Cody was different when they got him back. Among other things he wouldn't go in a crate and had anxiety issues. "Great," I said sarcastically. He was 115 pounds and all legs, tall like our Mastiff—and by tall I mean could easily reach the counter.

Joe, my husband, was all in, but I was very hesitant. The rescue had hired a professional trainer to work with the foster family to see if they could get Cody back in adoptable shape. We attended one of those training sessions, and on the drive home all I could think about were those BIG, potentially mud-filled paws and try not to cry.

How could we travel with a dog that refused to be crated? How could our aging neighbors and friends handle caring for such a big dog? Harvey was a

See what I mean?

breeze for them, which was so nice. He would just go to "Camp Watson," the neighbor's house, when we were gone.

In fact, one day we came home earlier than expected and my neighbor jokingly refused to give Harvey back—he really was the *best* dog ever!

What if Cody's anxiety didn't calm down? Those enormous paws could do a lot of damage quickly if he had motivation. Another problem behavior at his first "forever home" was that Cody was digging out of the yard. What if he tried to dig out of our house? And those enormous paws could transport a lot of dirt. Have I mentioned he had BIG PAWS? I was rather liking the break from constant cleaning while we were between dogs. What if we couldn't control him and learn to be "alpha?" Bottom line, I did not want Cody.

 But my husband TOTALLY did. Cody was *exactly* what he was looking for. Joe told me I could "veto," though how could I? He wanted that dog so badly. Say no to this dog, then go get one I liked? Seemed selfish. Joe had answers to all my concerns, but he's a "glass half full" kinda guy. His answer to "What if his anxiety doesn't get better?" was "It will." Ugh.

Since I couldn't bring myself to say yes, I dragged my heels—for like, two months! So, what I sensed God telling me here was, "Yes, Cody might, and probably will, destroy something you love—such as your mother-in-law's lamp or the program to your dad's funeral just to name a few. He's going to make traveling hard and more expensive. Those big paws are going to create a lot of work for you and make your floors dirty, especially your nice, clean carpet. Yes, entertaining will be challenging if you cannot crate Cody and he can reach all the food. In fact, you will need to completely rethink food storage in general. All the horrible things you are picturing may happen, but you can make a *choice* right here and now, *before* you start this story, to love Cody anyway."

I realize that God choosing to love us, and people making choices to love each other, are WAY bigger and more important concepts than my silly little dog dilemma. "First world problem," right? It might seem small to others, but this decision could be a ten-year commitment, and I truly struggled with it. I didn't want to adopt Cody, and I didn't want to disappoint Joe. I was stuck. I love that God cares about what concerns me and was faithful in giving me what I needed to make the decision. I was not quite able to say yes, so I told Joe that I "Wouldn't say no," and we adopted Cody.

Has Cody destroyed things? Yep! Does he make my carpet dirty? Yep—remind me to tell you about the time he had diarrhea *all over* my house which I came home to five minutes before expecting a guest. Unlike God's acceptance of us which is immediate, my acceptance of Cody was gradual. Sure, I accepted him in the house physically, but in the beginning, I would refer to Cody as "Joe's dog." I gradually dropped that terminology as God faithfully reminded me that I made a *choice* to love and accept him "anyway," and I am loving my husband by doing so. Have there been good times? Yes. Is his anxiety better? Yes—much! He eats everything in sight, and we don't entertain guests as often because of it. Do I enjoy him sometimes? Yes, he's growing on me.

Me and Cody

How about you? Anyone you could choose to "love anyway?" Consider quieting yourself for a moment and asking God if there are any relationships you've walked away from or closed off because they were unpleasant or too much work that He would like you to resume. Ask Him to reveal to you His heart for the relationship and how you can live that out in His strength. I can attest it sure helps to see things from His perspective—His perspective is what led me to accept Cody.

3

"Don't Do It, Cody"

There is a way which seems right to a person, But its end is the way of death. PROVERBS 14:12 NASB

Cody 'protecting' us from squirrels in the woodpile.

Our current dog Cody is more of an alpha than either of our previous pets, though in reading on that topic, I realized we allowed bad, disruptive, dominant behavior with our previous dog. Oops! Cody's dominant behavior was such a concern the rescue we adopted him from asked us to meet with a professional trainer they hired after his first adoption failed. I think this was a chance for us to assess what we were getting ourselves into and for them to evaluate whether we would be a good fit. When we first brought Cody home, we were very intentional about practicing alpha behaviors with him—showing him *we* were the pack leaders. We went through doors first. We ate first. He was on "heel" for part of our walks.

Initially, things went smoothly, but over time we got a little lazy—and by "we" I mean 30% me and 70% my husband—in my never-to-be-humble opinion. Cody started jumping, well, maybe lurching would be a better word, at trucks, buses, vans, and even other dogs while walking the neighborhood. Did I mention Cody is 130 pounds and tall like a deer? We—and by "we" I mostly mean me—assumed he was transitioning back to alpha and was being protective.

This was *not* desirable behavior. He could easily knock me over or pull me into oncoming traffic, and if not me, then one of our dog sitters who is at least ten years older than us. I kept picturing Cody wrapped around a school bus tire and ending up hurt or killed. If you are going to get injured while protecting us, Cody, can it be against an actual threat like a knife wielding intruder instead of a school bus?

I'm sure in his mind—yes, he's a dog acting on instinct and not "thinking," but bear with me here—Cody had a legitimate rationale. *That Amazon delivery van is a threat. I must protect my people.* My best guess—Cody didn't tell me.

Cody and I have a different perspective on this because, well, Cody's not human. We humans are a whole different species and on a higher intelligence level, able to see the bigger picture. School buses are *not* a threat but a great service to our community. That sweet little dog that wants to sniff him is *not* a threat but wanting to make friends. Cody might not understand it, but in most situations, *we* know better than *he* does what is best for him—don't chase that school bus because you could get run over, for example. Cody could walk a much calmer and safer path if he listened to *our* direction and rules and not what *he* thinks is best.

Could it be that some of God's guidelines we don't like or fully understand are the same way? That what "seems" right to us (*I need to get that bus*) might hurt us? That when God says "no," He means "don't hurt yourself?" Hmmm ... I kinda think so.

I can point to many times in life when I was tempted to solve issues my way but reluctantly—kicking, screaming, and pouting like a kid inside is more like it—obeyed God's guidelines. With the luxury of hindsight, I'm sooo thankful now as I can see how destructive doing things my way would have been.

What about you? Are you tempted to do something or head in a direction where God says, "No, that's not best for you," and you don't understand it or just plain don't want to? Can you see where His guidelines have protected you and your loved ones from heartache or harm? You might consider asking Him to show you some of these places if you don't see them.

4

Lord Make Me More Like...My Dog?

My boys in a bedtime hug

Love is patient, love is kind. It does
not envy, it does not boast, it is not
proud. It does not dishonor others,
it is not self-seeking, it is not eas-
ily angered, it keeps no record of
wrongs. It always protects, always
trusts, always hopes, always perse-
veres.
1 CORINTHIANS 13:4-5,7 NIV

To be honest, I wasn't quite sure what to write here, but how could I do a devotional about dogs and not comment on unconditional love? Sure, we all know dogs that, because of abuse or for whatever reason, do not fit this profile fully, but there is *absolutely* a reason dogs are known as "man's best friend."

How did they get that title, and why do we uphold them as a standard of unconditional love? I think one reason is that they are simple and don't overanalyze. They don't ascribe motives to our actions. We came home three hours late last night, which delayed Cody's dinner. I picture a human meeting us with a negative greeting such as, "Well it's about time. What kept you? Did you forget me?" But Cody was just happy to see us—met us at the door wagging his tail and holding a toy. He didn't pout or punish us later either. No hard feelings.

I've already stated that I did not want Cody, but he didn't know that. As he figured out Joe and I were his pack, he loved us consistently. He wanted to be with us, wanted to walk and explore with us, wanted us to pet him and snuggle. He barked at airplanes to protect us, and showed up at the door with tail wagging and holding a toy when we arrived home each day. How could that constant love and positivity not win me over? Reminds me of the way our heavenly Father consistently and sacrificially loves and pursues us.

Dogs can be better at patience than we are—happy to lie by our side for hours, stand up and stare at the ball for fifteen minutes, then lie by our side again quietly when we "didn't get the message." They seem to understand their part in the world and not overthink things—yes, different species, I know. Their lack of internal dialogue allows them to always be fully present and they are never too cool to fully express their love and happiness.

They don't play mind games. Okay, maybe that's not true. I swear Cody is staring at me right now trying to telepathically send a message, but I'm too dense to get it. For example, they don't say yes when they mean no. There's a sweet simplicity to their affection. It's honest, no grudges, no games, and a lot of dogs pretty much love everybody, too.

Well, I know I could *always* use a reminder to get out of my head, live in the present, assume the best about people, and love everybody. Any of that hit home with you today?

Prayer: Father, thank you for your unconditional love. Thank you for the reminder I see of it in my dog. Please, make me more like my dog.

"I've Got the Power!"

You are from God, little children,
and have overcome them; because
greater is He who is in you than he
who is in the world.
1 JOHN 4:4 NASB

Aslan contained by a simple screen

Now to Him who is able to do
far more abundantly beyond all
that we ask or think, according to
the power that works within us ...
EPHESIANS 3:20 NASB

This is Aslan, our first dog. We named him after the lion character from C.S. Lewis' Chronicles of Narnia because both of his parents were over 200 pounds and, at a quick glance, they looked more like lions than dogs to us. It's hard to believe he was only eight pounds when we brought him home. Runt of the litter—I love a bargain. We used to laugh because he was HUGE yet so easy to contain. If you left a door cracked open, he would look through it, but if he couldn't fit, he made no attempt to push it. The dog could literally breathe on the thing and move it, but he just never discovered his power. It seemed so ironic given his size. Crazy! The disconnect between his potential abilities or power and lack of engagement with them was stunning.

Note in the picture above we simply leaned the screen from a window over the opening to the porch and it kept him contained. My point is that he had *no idea* of his power. He weighed 195 pounds. He could push, scratch, eat, and again, practically just blow on that screen to get out if he wanted, but he never tried. While very convenient for us that Aslan did not know his power, it also seemed a bit sad.

Spiritually, I'm the same way at times. I am continually surprised and disappointed with how long it takes me to engage the power I have in Christ and through prayer invite God into my challenges—however big or small. Sometimes it's the small, nagging issues that don't seem big enough to rise to the level of a prayer request. I remember struggling with a headache all day and medication was not helping, but mid-afternoon for some reason it dawned on me to pray about it, and poof! No headache. Why did that not occur to me earlier? Now, of course, that quick response doesn't always happen. Darn.

What about you? Are there places in your life you feel stuck, trapped, isolated, restrained? Problems you've forgotten to invite God into? How does it change the way you look at things to meditate on the fact that the *same power* that raised Jesus from the dead lives in you? Jesus says in Matthew 28 that all power and authority in Heaven and Earth has been given to Him and He will be with us.

I encourage you to be mindful of the power you carry, and to invite God into your stuck places. I know I can always use the reminder! What if the breakthrough you need is as easy as my dog Aslan gently blowing on that screen and knocking it over—you just haven't engaged your powerhouse? Let's spend some time talking to "Him who is able to do far more abundantly beyond all that we ask or imagine."

You CAN Teach an Old Dog New Tricks!

> *See to it that no one takes you captive through hollow and deceptive philosophy, which depends on human tradition and the elemental spiritual forces of this world rather than on Christ.*
> **COLOSSIANS 2:8 NIV**

Aslan in his later years

E verybody knows you can't teach an old dog new tricks, right? *Everybody* knows that. I mean, we've all heard the saying and the saying had to come from somewhere, so it must be true. Except it's not. Many years ago, I visited a friend at her farm. I love horses. This gave me the opportunity to be around them as well as see my friend. She had several dogs, and I remember being impressed that she had taught one of her dogs to "shake it off" on command. Upon hearing the order, her black lab would shake all over like dogs do when coming out of the water to dry off. It seemed like a hard trick to teach, AND she taught her dog this when he was a senior. Whaaaat? This challenged my belief system.

I enjoyed teaching our dogs to do tricks, and I like teaching them unique ones. My Mastiff, Aslan, was also a senior at this time. I hadn't tried to teach him anything new in a few years—because, *everybody* knows "you can't teach an old dog new tricks." I decided to teach Aslan to "flap your ears." My husband was on board, so we started giving Aslan the command, then rubbing under his ears to encourage the action, and then praising the correct response. We repeated this multiple times a day for what seemed like forever.

There were days I thought he was never going to get it. Maybe her dog was smarter. Maybe my dog was senile and had dementia. Maybe "they" were right about old dogs' ability to learn. It definitely took longer than other tricks he'd learned, but one day—he did it! Though shaky at first, ultimately, our old dog learned the new trick of "flap your ears!"

So, what does this mean? Well first of all, "they" were wrong! Who exactly are "they" anyway? What other things might "they"—or the world—be wrong about? We do unconsciously agree with a lot of ideas that the world throws at us. The thoughts seem to have always been with us, and they "feel" true and familiar.

But some of these thoughts are *not* true and believing them holds us back from reaching our full potential. What if Aslan had never learned to "flap your ears?" Okay, that was supposed to be a joke because it would have been no big deal, but in *our* lives, not learning new tricks or traveling new roads can have significant consequences. It can hold us back from stepping into who we were meant to be, from trying new things, from experiencing true joy and satisfaction.

Take a few minutes and ask the Lord to reveal any areas where you have accepted false ideas that hold you back. I'll get you started, but feel free to just sit quietly and ask the Lord to speak to you directly.

Try filling in the blanks:

I'll never _____

I am _____

I can't _____

God is _____

God won't _____

They think I _____

Aslan taking a break from learning new tricks

7

Persistence

Be persistent in prayer, and keep
alert as you pray, giving thanks to
God. COLOSSIANS 4:2 GNT

Cody asking for a road trip

> *... praying at all times in the Spirit, with all prayer and supplication. To that end, keep alert with all perseverance, making supplication for all the saints ...*
> EPHESIANS 6:18 ESV

My current dog, Cody, knows what suitcases mean. The picture above is Cody helping us by preemptively loading himself in the car, so we don't forget him on our trip. So helpful, right? Except Cody couldn't go with us this time. Good try, Cody! My husband would say, "Keep hope alive." For not speaking the English language, dogs can sure communicate quite well, can't they?

This next picture is Cody clearly communicating to me he would like to join me on an adventure. I had stopped at home to drop off groceries before running out and finishing a few more errands. As I unloaded the car, Cody jumped in the back and made it clear he was not being left behind! Now, to be fair, I could have *made* him get out, but I felt a bit sorry for him and my "down" commands were a little half-hearted.

I decided to see how long his determination would last. With the garage closed to the street, I left the back of the vehicle open and started putting away the groceries in the house. I thought he would come in after a few minutes, but can you believe after twenty-five minutes he was still in the car?

His persistence impressed me enough that I decided to postpone my errands, and we went to the dog park. (Yay for Cody!). This reminds me of the New Testament story in Luke 18 about the persistent widow. Jesus describes a woman who keeps pestering a judge regarding her case. The judge admits that he doesn't fear God or care what other people think, but he grants her request, so she won't cause trouble for him later. He just wants her to go away. Jesus then asks how much more will God who loves us, and cares about us, reward our persistence? I don't think Jesus is saying ask for whatever you want—if you ask Him daily for a Porsche, you might get it. But He *is* sharing an example of rewarding persistence. I didn't plan to take Cody to the park, but because of his persistence, I rewarded him.

There is another story in Matthews 15 where a Canaanite woman is following Jesus and His disciples asking for help with her demon possessed daughter. Jesus ignores her, and the disciples ask Him to send her away. But she is persistent. Jesus puts her off twice—at first saying He was only sent to the Jews, and next saying, "It is not good to take the children's bread and throw it to the dogs." Don't read that as an insult. Jesus was testing her faith. She replies, "Yes Lord, but even the dogs feed on the crumbs which fall from their master's table." He is impressed with her answer and doggedness, and heals her daughter immediately. What if she had given up after Jesus ignored her? Or, after His first "you are not important" comment (my paraphrase). No healing!

I've rejoiced over answered prayers that have been a LOOOONG time coming! Requests that not only went unanswered, but for *so long* I saw no movement, lost hope, and stopped praying—until God reminded me to be persistent, and the concerns went back on my list. It's so satisfying to have answers to those requests. It gives me hope for others that have not been answered, yet. I know all my prayers may not be answered in the way I desire, but I'm thankful for His reminders to me about being consistent in lifting my requests to Him, and for His faithfulness.

Have you seen the reward of persistence? Are there any good things you've given up praying about that you need to rewrite on your list? God encourages persistence. Ask Him if there is an area you could be more faithful about lifting up to Him. You are dearly loved, precious ones.

8

Crazy Prayer

*You do not have because you do not
ask God.* JAMES 4:2b NIV

Aslan enjoying a rare snowstorm

A righteous person has regard
for the life of his animal ...
PROVERBS 12:10a NASB

Have you ever asked God for healing? How about healing your pet? Do you think that's silly? Do you think God doesn't care about our animals? I'm guessing if you've chosen to read this book, there's a good chance you think He does.

As a puppy, our first dog, Aslan, gave us multiple scares with limping after flying across the kitchen floor chasing a ball. Sadly, he was our only dog that would chase a ball. We would hurry to the vet worried something was broken only to be assured it was a sprain and that he would recover.

A few years later, he had another incident which caused him to limp for a while. This time the vet said they didn't know what it was and gave him the diagnosis of panosteitis. I remember thinking, *I've taken medical terminology. I know that simply means "swelling around the joint." Are you just trying to give me an official sounding name to make me happy and go away?* More importantly, though, this time they did *not* assure us he would recover and indicated it might be a permanent condition.

I was devastated. He was too young to be permanently injured! He weighed 195 pounds which is a lot on those legs, and if one was gimpy, could that not impact his lifespan?

I'm almost embarrassed to share this because it sounds goofy. This is the moment when people think, "Hmm, I thought she was normal but wow, she really is a little crazy." Anyway, here goes. I believe the Spirit prompted me to pray for Aslan's healing. Why do I say this? Because I doubt it would have occurred to me naturally. I'd never heard of or seen anyone pray for animal healings as we do for humans. There are no examples of this in scripture, and after all, he was "only a dog." It seemed bold and maybe a bit selfish to ask for this. Not only was I prompted to lay hands on Aslan and pray for his healing, but also to tell people that I did it—sort of putting it out there as a step of faith. I remember feeling conflicted. At times I was embarrassed about it, but at other moments I didn't care what people thought. This was not my natural inclination and felt uncomfortable. It would have been easier to just pray, hope, and never tell anyone so I wasn't "that crazy lady."

Well, it wasn't an instant healing, and you can debate me about natural healing versus God's intervention if you want; I can be tempted to debate that myself. What I remember is several days after this noticing that Aslan had completely recovered—and being shocked. Next, I was disappointed in myself for being so shocked! Had I not prayed about this? Why was I surprised that my prayer was answered? Fighting the temptation to doubt, I chose to give God glory and thank Him for it.

For me, the lesson in this was that God *does* care about the "little" things, that God *does* still do miracles. Part of man's role as stewards of the Earth is taking care of its creatures, and this was an example of acting in that role. You can say I'm silly, but I know in my heart He was building my faith. It also served to grow my ability to listen for His voice and direction, and to obey even though it seemed odd or uncomfortable.

Is there something you think is too small, silly, or out of bounds to pray for? Are you tempted to think God really doesn't do miracles anymore? Is there something your heart really wants, but you are afraid to put it out there and ask for? Take a deep breath in and blow it out slowly. Ask God about this and see what comes to mind.

Aslan as a puppy

9

Just Because

Aslan 'shaking' for a treat

... to redeem those under the law, that we might receive adoption to sonship. Because you are his sons, God sent the Spirit of his Son into our hearts, the Spirit who calls out, "Abba, Father." So you are no longer a slave, but God's child; and since you are his child, God had made you also an heir.

GALATIANS 4:5-7 NIV

Please answer the following questions. Don't overthink it. Go with the first thought that comes to mind.

1) Does God love you? Yes / No.

2) Does God accept you? Yes / No.

3) What makes you acceptable to God?

Putting our faith in Jesus and His sacrifice as atonement for our sins gets us adopted into His family. What place does doing good deeds have in the kingdom? I would like to suggest our good deeds are a response to God's lavish love for us and *not* an attempt to get His continued approval which we *already have*. Yet, I can be tempted to feel like I still have to have good behavior for God to love and accept me. I see others mistakenly thinking the same thing, too. Please do not assume that I am saying our behavior doesn't matter and has no consequences. That's NOT what I'm saying.

Our behavior *does* have consequences—to our intimacy with God, to our witness for the kingdom, to our relationship with others on Earth, to our life and situation on Earth. Murder someone: go to jail. Tell lies and gossip: see how many people want to be your friend, or ever trust you, and wonder why you are lonely. When Christians' behavior does not line up with the biblical teaching they ascribe to, no wonder many people find it unattractive and are not interested in sharing that same faith.

However, I *don't* think the consequences to our behavior look like this: tell lies and gossip—all listed as sins in the Bible—and God does not accept you. Go stand in the corner and skip dinner as punishment. Or He lets bad things happen to you as a result. Instead, I think God's heart is sad when you feel you need to lie and gossip to feel good about yourself or fix your problems, and He wishes you would bring them to Him instead and trust Him more. You could live in greater freedom and experience greater joy. He longs for you to walk in that.

And while the Bible does talk about running for the prize and receiving crowns, I don't believe our behavior changes His *acceptance* of us. He has no teacher's pets. Working hard for His approval by perfect church attendance, teaching Sunday School, and helping old ladies across the street does not earn you a bigger smile and extra scoops of ice cream at dinner. If you have joined the family, you have His full love and acceptance—and all the ice cream you want.

I enjoy teaching my dogs to do tricks. I love to interact and communicate with them. I find pleasure in seeing the gleam in their eyes as they eagerly anticipate the treat, in watching them focus and learn, and rewarding their success. With our second dog, Harvey, it started to seem like the *only* time he got treats was when doing tricks. This didn't feel right. He should get good things just for being a part of our household and not have to earn them.

Because of this, we added another trick. After he performed all his current tricks, I started asking him to— wait for it —"Harvey ... be cute!" Long dramatic pause as he maintained his focus on me and the treat. Then, "Oh—GOOD BOY!" I would give him the treat.

In doing this we were saying, "You don't always have to earn good things in this household. You are a part of the pack. This is a good pack, and you get good things just because we love you. Just because." We didn't want Harvey to think he had to earn our affection or good things like treats.

Now, we didn't love *all* of Harvey's behavior, and there were consequences to his undesired actions. Jump on our bed: when caught be scolded and told to get down, *now*. If Harvey had continued this behavior, he might have been restricted to the first floor while we were gone. Does this mean we did not accept Harvey? No. Did he have to do ten good things or tricks before he was viewed as "acceptable" again? No. He became accepted when we adopted him into our pack, and his behavior did not change that.

How do you feel when you think about Father God? There is a line in a devotional I love that says, "See me seeing you." If you close your eyes and picture Father God looking at you right now, what do you see? What is His posture? What is His expression? Is He smiling at you? What is He thinking? If this is uncomfortable for you and you are resisting, this may be a good exercise to come back to. If you don't see a gracious father who loves and accepts you despite your behavior—though He may want to have a noncondemning discussion with you about it—you might want to keep talking to Him about that. You are not a little dog constantly doing tricks for his master to get acceptance and treats. Harvey— BE CUTE! GOOD BOY!

And come on, wasn't Harvey just the cutest dog ever?

10

Aslan's Comfort

*My sheep listen to my voice; I know
them, and they follow me.*
JOHN 10:27 NIV

Aslan asking for an ear rub

God is our refuge and strength,
an ever-present help in trouble.
PSALM 46:1 NIV

When Aslan, our first dog, was ten and a half years old, our vet diagnosed him with a tumor. We chose not to have it removed because of his advanced age. During this time, I woke up one morning and realized my husband had not come to bed. At first, I was angry, suspecting he had irresponsibly stayed up all night—and on a work night, too. I went downstairs and found him sleeping on the couch next to Aslan who couldn't move his back legs and couldn't get comfortable. It was a clear sign it was time to put him down since at 195 pounds we could not carry him outside by ourselves to do his business.

The vet could not come until the afternoon, so I had to make it through a half day of work which seemed to never end. When the vet arrived, it was time to say goodbye to our sweet boy. It was a tender and tearful gathering of friends and neighbors. We all cried and shared stories of Aslan's adventures.

People were so sweet, loving, and supportive. They sent cards and called to check up on me, asking how I was doing and if I needed anything. I could tell they sincerely wanted to be there as a shoulder to lean on during this difficult time.

But I came away from some of those interactions feeling—I'm not sure exactly. Like I let them down, maybe. Like they expected me to fall apart and need them more than I did—that their expectations were not met.

Now there could have been unhealthiness on both sides here. I admit I may have been stuffing my emotions. I remember getting yelled at as a kid for crying when I found the dead body of our iguana while picking apples. That summer we had set Iggy, the iguana, outside in a makeshift cage that blew down, and we never found him—until picking apples that fall. It was traumatic as I literally went to grab the branch and my hand landed on what remained of Iggy. I cried. Dad grabbed me and shook me, yelling disgustedly that we "don't cry over dead animals." So, that may have taught me not to show my emotions about Alsan's passing.

I also have an unhealthy desire to not need other people. I like being independent and not "needy," which seems weak to me. I'm not saying this is good; I'm just acknowledging it. I think a few of the people who tried to be there for me may have the opposite unhealthy desire: the need to help others so they themselves feel valued. This in general is not bad, but what I sensed was a "I need you to need me so I can feel good about helping or fixing you." Can you see how their unhealthy desire to be helpful and my unhealthy desire to not need help might have led to some disappointing interactions?

Being unsettled, I decided to seek the Lord. I found a quiet place and asked Him something like this: "People want to help me through this grief, but it feels a bit empty. You are our comforter—is there something You have for me, Lord?"

Soon I envisioned a large field filled with tall grass waving in the wind. A huge lion walked slowly toward me. I immediately recognized him as the other Aslan, the God figure in *The Chronicles of Narnia*. He halted before me and looked down at me as I returned His gaze with reverence and awe. Aslan looked deep into my eyes and said with a strong, authoritative, yet loving and gentle voice, "You shepherded him well, Daughter of Eve."

Something broke in me. This declaration affirmed something I didn't know I needed to hear, but it settled something in my spirit and brought tears to my eyes. It was a deep, spirit level comfort I needed but others couldn't give me. I hugged Aslan and rested my head against His mane.

My point here is *not* that we shouldn't be there for each other. We were meant for community, and God *will* use people to comfort one another. We can and should provide support, listen to each other, and be a shoulder to cry on. There is nothing wrong with that. But God just "gets us" and knows our deepest need in a way others sometimes cannot. I don't always remember to turn to Him for comfort but was so glad and so blessed when I did that time.

What are you carrying that you could hand over to Jesus? If you think about it for a moment, can you see places of hunger in your life that you've tried to fill with what the world offers, but you aren't truly satisfied? Have you talked to Jesus about it? Consider doing that now.

11

Exposed

For the moment, all discipline seems not to be pleasant, but painful; yet to those who have been trained by it, afterward it yields the peaceful fruit of righteousness.
HEBREWS 12:11 NASB

Harvey shaved when we first adopted him and then with full-length hair

O ur second dog, Harvey, was a rescue. The story goes that he was taken from a hoarder who had 162 cats and eight dogs. One of my friends ended up fostering him. Supposedly, his hair was so matted and knotted that it restricted his movement, and he had to have it all shaved. He looked like a scrawny lion when we first saw him. He also looked a bit awkward and exposed without his hair (I'm sure it had *nothing* to do with his new surroundings, but let's blame it on the hair). I *swear* Harvey looked embarrassed at times that he didn't have all his clothes on.

He eventually did grow his fur back, but it took a while. It got me to thinking, occasionally we have to be willing to be a bit uncomfortable and exposed to move into places of greater freedom. I bet Harvey didn't *want* his hair shaved. I suspect he felt awkward and afraid. He probably couldn't fully remember what it felt like to move freely anyway, so he didn't know what he was missing or what real freedom felt like. Then the shears! Oh no! And he's surrounded by strangers. And he's cold. And he doesn't have the same familiar smells around him (like cat pee—gross!) But after the shave, "I can stretch out my legs again. Wow! I can reach my paw to scratch my ear, and it doesn't cause a sharp pain in my stomach, and I can actually reach my ear! *This* is what it feels like to really run!"

For Harvey, a season of discomfort and newness led to freedom. I've seen the same in my own life. At one point, God indicated He wanted me to get help addressing issues of abandonment and rejection stemming from my adoption and my many years of stuttering. I debated what form this help should take and settled on classes at a local counseling office that came with mentoring sessions. I always dreaded the mentoring sessions. At first it was just awkward as my mentor didn't provide much structure and just let me talk, which I resisted. Asking clarification questions on the teaching material didn't take much time. I stalled. I knew God called me to this and intellectually knew it would be freeing, but I didn't want to relive painful memories and the feelings of embarrassment and shame that accompanied them. I finally gave in and let her walk with me through some of these memories and let the Lord speak to me about them in prayer and, of course, it was wonderfully freeing. I walked out of those sessions feeling so much lighter. Leaving my comfort zone and exposing some deeply buried pain with His guidance ultimately led to greater joy and freedom.

Consider asking God if there are new places He is inviting you into, but you are refusing to go because you are unwilling to be uncomfortable. Maybe He will give you a glimpse of how being unrestrained in this area could look or feel. Are you willing to be uncomfortable to grow into new places of freedom knowing the One doing the shearing loves you dearly and desires the best for you?

Another Before and After

Harvey with his hair starting to grow back.
Look at that adorable face!

Harvey with his glorious, full coat of fur

12

I Did NOT Sign Up for This!

Joe and "Joe's dog," Cody

Therefore, I urge you, brothers and sisters, in view of God's mercy, to offer your bodies as a living sacrifice, holy and pleasing to God—this is your true and proper worship. ROMANS 12:1 NIV

@#!! I said $@%#! You @#&! dog! OMG. I was SOOOOOO MAD. Okay, in all honesty, I was really hurt, scared, and embarrassed. Had anyone seen that? I should not have held on to the leash or tried so hard to hold on to Cody. Let him get free and get hit by a car for all I cared at the moment. Did I really just think that? That's awful. I'm awful.

We had just exited the dog park—and we left early because Cody wouldn't leave some newbie alone. She didn't know you weren't supposed to bring treats in and acted annoyed that my *very* food motivated dog wouldn't stop following her. Hello? Really?

It was a beautiful spring day, just starting to dry out after a period of rain. I wanted Cody to get more exercise and I wanted to stay out longer, too. I had heard about a walking trail that led to a pond nearby and decided to explore it.

We had just strolled past the pond where the trail came to an end, and the land sloped upward toward a row of houses. I prepared to turn around, but Cody decided to *turbo* up the hill onto private property. I slid in the mud trying to hold him back while yelling, "NO!" Eventually a tree came to my rescue and snagged the leash, slowing him down and turning him around.

On the way back, I paused to let him drink in the pond and as he trotted up the bank and headed down the trail, he decided again to give it all the *turbo* power he had. One might argue that I should have anticipated this given he had just done the same thing a few minutes earlier, but these spurts of energy were unusual for him, so, alas, I did not. Okay, maybe I'm being a little dramatic here, but I *swear* I was airborne for five feet, meaning five feet high *and then* propelled five feet forward before hitting the ground and being dragged. I'm still not sure what made him stop, but I screamed "NO! $@&♂^*!!" When he finally stopped, he looked back at me as if saying, "What's your problem? That was fun. Let's do it again!"

I was SOOO MAD. I was SOOOO MAD! What was I? MAD! Oh, and scared, and embarrassed, too, but **MAD** felt so much tougher.

I don't get mad like that very often. Really. According to a free online personality test, I'm an Enneagram Type 9 people pleaser which means I don't get mad. People don't like that. It's not *pleasing* to be around. So, when I had time to think about my reaction, what was really going on?

I was afraid, and I had not fully surrendered Cody to God when I first said yes to him. When I agreed to "love Cody anyway" I anticipated he might damage my stuff, destroy my house, make it dirty, eat a couch, cost me money, and make it difficult to travel, whatever, but I was *not* ready for him to hurt me physically. Had that ground not been soft from rain (thank you for the mud, God?) I could easily have been badly injured. I'm rather surprised I didn't break my wrist I landed so hard. I thought I had surrendered Cody and all his potential bad behavior, but I was *not prepared* and would NEVER forgive Cody —or Joe— if *his* dog caused me physical harm.

Bottom line, it came down to expectations and surrender. "God, I thought I was ready for all the bad things Cody could do, but this was *not* on my preapproved list of Cody problems. I am not willing to have a significant physical injury because of him. I'm prepared to sacrifice my property but *not* my physical well-being. You and I had an agreement.

What? You mean we didn't? You mean when You told me to love Cody anyway and I agreed, it could include this? Okay, I'm out. I'm never walking *Joe's dog*—I mean Cody—again."

Have you ever said yes to God thinking you were agreeing to one thing and found the situation wasn't what you expected? How did that go for you? I bet after disappointment and accepting the new circumstances it became an opportunity for growth. My only path back to peace was to forgive Joe. Yes, illogical, but I felt it was his fault in a roundabout way. Then I needed to surrender my rights as well as my expectations about the way rescuing Cody would look.

If you are brave and have decided in advance you will obey whatever God tells you, consider asking Him to reveal any boundaries or limits you've drawn that He would like to erase. Write them down. Now for the hard part—surrender them. Freedom awaits!

13

Shut Your Mouth!!

*My dear brothers and sisters, take
note of this: Everyone should be
quick to listen, slow to speak and
slow to become angry,*
JAMES 1:19 NIV

Cody in "time out"

Those who guard their mouths
and their tongues keep themselves
from calamity.
PROVERBS 21:23 NIV

W ant to talk about it?

That's all Joe said. He had come home and could tell something was amiss because Cody was locked up in the office, his time out place, with the gate closed. Cody had already earned "whole house privileges" even when we were away.

"Nope!" I said, fighting back tears.

Remember the adventure at the dog park? Well, that day just got better and better! Yes, sarcasm. Upon arriving home, I put Cody in the office to give myself time to cool down. When I did release him, he was only out for approximately fifteen minutes before I heard noises downstairs. He had chosen this day, *this day*, when I was already so VERY happy with his behavior, to jump up on the tall buffet table and retrieve two small, dry dog biscuits that had been there for *weeks* untouched. In the process, he knocked other items off, and might have tried tasting the candles that fell, too.

Sure, in his defense, he was probably wound up and anxious, sensing my mood, and I *did* put the treats there, but I would argue that I considered them high enough to be out of reach, knowing he could easily reach the kitchen counter.

Anyway, back to the office he went. Gate closed and I ignored him. I was done!

Joe was being sweet and did *really* want to know what had happened, but I still believe it was wise to keep my mouth shut. I might have been holding back tears, but I knew the moment my mouth started moving I wouldn't be able to control the stream of angry, hurtful, words I couldn't take back.

It probably would have started with my yelling at the top of my lungs "YOUR DOG!" And it would have been emotional, and loud, and hurtful, and involve blaming. I would have been the innocent, wronged party, of course. And—It would have been very *unproductive*. I'm so glad I kept my mouth zipped that night. Don't for a moment be impressed because I'm not always able to restrain myself. Sometimes I say the stuff I really shouldn't and regret it later.

How do you deal with this? It's HARD, isn't it? Lashing out can feel good in the moment, but quickly we realize we're hurting people we love. When I'm protecting *myself*, I forget that I'm attacking and injuring someone *else*. Oops. Our words are powerful. They can serve to bless people and bring them together, or cause division. Loud, angry words do not build intimacy or trust in a relationship—and therefore do not ultimately accomplish any of my long-term goals. Does this bring to mind anything you want to confess or talk to God about involving your words? "He is faithful to forgive us ...."

14

Walking in the Spirit

Samson walking in perfect heel

If we live by the Spirit, let's follow
the Spirit as well.
GALATIANS 5:25 NASB

What does it mean to "walk in the Spirit?" Someone posed this question in a Bible study, and I immediately pictured a man walking with his dog on the greenway near my house. The owner had a huge Great Dane that walked off leash in perfect heel. The man carried a short leash, but I never saw him use it. The dog walked quietly by his side. When the owner stopped, the dog stopped. It was so unique the first few times I saw the pair I wondered if the owner might be advertising a dog training company. As they ambled down the trail, the dog took in the scenery around him, every now and then glancing at his owner. The dog seemed comfortable to let you pet him (after asking the owner of course), but his focus remained centered on his master —or at least his attention was divided and tuned in to his owner even while I petted him.

Isn't this a good picture of walking in the Spirit? A dog performing "heel" correctly should match his master's pace. If the master speeds up, so should the dog. If the master stops, slows down, or changes direction, so should the dog. The dog isn't staring at the master the whole time. He walks next to him, looking forward but still so aware of what the master is doing that he can adjust. If something really interesting, or a potential threat, pops into the dog's awareness, like a rabbit or another dog, he may perk up, but he checks in with the master before responding. The master may release him from heel to chase the rabbit or keep him on heel, and the dog obeys. He trusts the master and can relax and obey from this place of trust.

To be honest, this dog stood out to me because so few dogs do this well. Seems like what I most commonly see are dogs who cannot contain themselves, who must explore all distractions and chase all threats.

What does this look like in humans? Personally, I think a good "walking in the Spirit" day is not when I'm in a daylong quiet time. Instead, I'm doing my usual activities, but with an awareness that I am connected spiritually to God. If a threat approaches, usually in the form of a lie or false belief, or I must decide how to respond to others, I am continually having a side conversation with God. *What do you say about that?*

How do you want me to respond to this person? Say yes or no? Listen only, or speak truth gently in love? God speak through me. God love them through me. Then I believe that He will do it, trusting Him to know how to protect me and respond best to others. I trust He knows all and wants only my good.

The days I am *not* walking in the Spirit, though, look very different. I may not need to describe this to you though as flesh behavior is easily recognizable. For me it looks like me being easily offended, critical, and controlling. These are the days I don't keep my mouth shut and say things I shouldn't, trying to fix people and protect myself.

Ask God to grow your ability to recognize and listen to the Spirit today. Consider starting your day by surrendering it to Him. Intentionally ask the Spirit to guide and direct you—and remind you to check in with Him. Then walk forward trusting He will do it. At the end of the day, look back. How was it different than other days? Ask Him to show where you got it right.

My friend Lauren and Remi walking a beautiful heel

15

Giving Grace to Rescues

Be kind to one another, compassionate, forgiving each other, just as God in Christ also has forgiven you. EPHESIANS 4:32 NASB

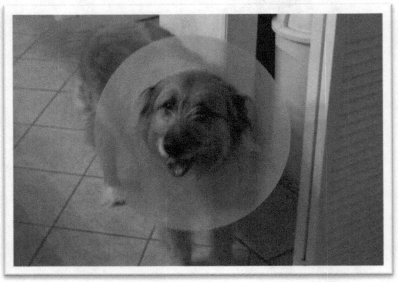

Harvey, our first rescue

Above all, love each other deeply,
because love covers over a multi-
tude of sins. 1 PETER 4:8 NIV

Have you ever been in public and watched someone approach a dog only to have the dog bark, or run and hide behind its owner? What starts as noise and hiding can quickly turn into snapping or attempting to bite the stranger.

What often happens next is the owner apologizes and explains something along these lines, "I'm sorry but Snoopy here is a rescue. He was abused or neglected," or "We don't know what happened to Snoopy, but she doesn't like men." At that point, some people will walk away, but others become more determined to gain Snoopy's trust. They give the dog a compassionate look, bend down to get on the dog's level, and continue talking to the owner giving Snoopy time to warm up to them. If available, they might give the dog a treat while avoiding eye contact in the hopes that Snoopy will be brave and come out from hiding. These are folks willing to painstakingly sacrifice both time and effort to try to win the dog over.

What if humans gave each other the same grace? You get rude treatment from a server at a restaurant and instead of walking out saying, "What a jerk," you continue to treat them with kindness. You try even harder to connect—look them straight in the eye and ask about their day. You still give them a tip.

They don't have someone standing alongside them to tell you, "They are tired from burning the candle at both ends and caring for an aging parent." "They were just diagnosed with cancer." "Their parents told them they were stupid and would never amount to anything, and they lack self-confidence though it comes across as being rude."

It seems to me that very much like dogs, humans tend to be a product of their environment. We don't wake up *wanting* to be mean and hurt those around us, and when we do, it is often a form of learned behavior or self-protection.

Would the world not be a better place if we gave each other the same grace and nonjudgmental posture we give these dogs? Sure, we don't have someone giving us the details, but can we pause and remember that ugly behavior usually comes from ugly circumstances and experiences? Can we take a deep breath and give them grace—but even more than that, intentionally be kind to them? Could we even think about being a small part of a healing moment that just maybe enables them to trust people more and put down the protective mechanisms? What would that world look like?

Does someone come to mind as you read this to whom you could be more intentional about loving and not holding a grudge against?

I admit when I started writing this day's devotional, I struggled to remember a personal example, but God is good!

I was shopping at a local grocery store and ordering food from the deli. I hate to cook. While I cannot recall the exact details of the encounter, I *do* remember the guy behind the counter being *so rude* to me. I was only ordering food. "Can I have a pound of that and a half a pound of that?" What did I do? I cannot believe I gave him any legitimate reason to be rude, but from my perspective he was obnoxious and, yes, it bothered me, and it hurt, and I felt rejected—all that good stuff you are supposed to be over as an adult, right?

While shopping there recently, I deliberately avoided ordering food because I didn't want to deal with him. Okay, let's be real—I didn't want to be hurt again. I considered waiting in line and, if it was his turn to help me, requesting someone *else* serve me to make a point, maybe hurt him back a little? But I didn't. I just left.

The next time I visited, I decided I would not avoid him but intentionally make eye contact and be kind. I can't say it went perfectly, but I did my part. That was my chance to practice. What about you? Who has been weird, awkward, mean, or rude to you that you can practice being intentional about "loving anyway" and not holding a grudge or being hurt by them? "They will know we are Christians by our love ...."

Another cute Harvey pic. I couldn't help myself.

16

What You Focus On You Give Power To

Cody waiting for a treat

I keep my eyes always on the Lord.
With him at my right hand, I will
not be shaken. PSALM 16:8 NIV

E ver tried to teach your dog the "leave it" command? They say it is
one of the easiest to teach. You place a treat in front of them, tell
them to "leave it," but keep your hand close by so when they go for the
treat you can cover it and say "no." When they pull their nose away, you
give them positive feedback and let them have the treat. They quickly
learn what you are asking for, so you don't have to guard the treat so
closely and can gradually work on lengthening the time they wait.

Cody was usually pretty solid with this trick. One day while working
on it, the first time I put the treat in front of him and told him to "leave
it," he kept his gaze fixed on the treat. He held out for five to ten seconds
but couldn't wait until I gave him the "okay" signal, and he ate it too
soon. "No, Cody!" The treat was too enticing.

We tried again and this time, instead of looking at the treat, he looked
at me while waiting and, to my surprise, he resisted until I gave him the
release which was at least twice the time if not longer. I've noticed since
then that not only does he do much better and is able to resist temptation
when he is looking at *me* rather than the treat, but when I notice his
resolve weakening and his eyes start wandering down, if I talk to him
("good boy, Cody; you're doing great") it helps him stay strong, refocus
on me, and hang in there. We just tried again while I'm writing this so I
could take a picture, and he held out for a full minute.

"Good job, Cody!"

What a beautiful picture of us and our "heavenly Master." When we
are tempted by something, do we do better when we focus on the thing

or on Jesus? We cannot always control what temptations come our way, but we *can* control what we look at and think about. Listening to Jesus while we are focusing on Him, and not the temptation, is even better.

Practical applications? When I'm trying to give up sugar or junk food, it sure is easier not to have it in the house, and I'm thankful I don't sit by the snack area at work. Plus, my goal today was to not have sugar until dessert tonight after dinner, but wow, writing this with the awareness of what is in my pantry is *not* helping my resolve. How about less concrete, inner temptations? When I am struggling to stand in truth, I often write out scriptures and carry them with me to review several times a day, sometimes hourly, to refocus my thoughts and attention. It works!

Where might this apply to you? Mentally list your current struggles or temptations. Have you invited Jesus into them and asked Him for wisdom? How much of your time is spent gazing at these problems rather than Him? What can you do to shift that focus?

17

Holy Spirit Leading

But the Helper, the Holy Spirit whom the Father will send in My name, He will teach you all things, and remind you of all that I said to you. JOHN 14:26 NASB

Cody pointing toward his bowl hinting it's dinnertime

After the earthquake came a fire,
but the Lord was not in the fire.
And after the fire came a gentle
whisper. I KINGS 19:12 NIV

I am concerned some of you will find this sacrilegious, but I want to make an analogy between the Holy Spirit and my dog. Many people tell me they cannot hear God. Some say the Holy Spirit is a gentleman in that He will lead you but never force you to see or do anything. I believe scripture indicates we have a part to play in being guided by the Holy Spirit which includes waiting and watching for Him. Our job is to seek.

When I think of the Holy Spirit leading like a gentleman, I think of my current dog. Cody is not very talkative. He doesn't vocalize or bark much, and sometimes he can slink around unnoticed despite his large size. One minute he's not there and the next minute you look up—surprise—there he is lying a few feet away. I guess what I'm saying here is he doesn't always *announce* himself. He doesn't demand my attention.

Cody sleeps on his own bed in our bedroom. In the mornings, when the alarm goes off or is about to, Cody knows it's time for food and a walk. He will reposition himself with his head toward the bedroom door. He doesn't bark or whine. He may walk around a bit if he thinks we are not moving fast enough, but if we don't get up, eventually he just lays down and waits.

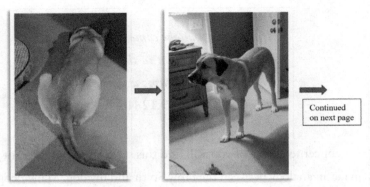

Continued
on next page

Cody's progression of "guiding" us in our morning routine

The minute we get out of bed, he makes his next move. He slides to the hallway. He'll stand and look back to see if we are following. He may walk back and forth a few times to communicate to us "come this way," but if we are too slow, he will lay down in the hall, body pointed toward the stairs, looking back, and watching us. If he notices we are paying him attention, or we take a step toward the door, he will move closer to the stairs—giving us our next clue to the direction he would like us to go.

Cody knows the *correct* plan is to go down the stairs, and if I deviate to do ironing in the guest bedroom first, he won't come in with me. Instead, he stays out in the hall, so he's close by, easily found, and positioned between me and the right direction—meaning filling his food bowl.

He likes to do this at his dinnertime, too. He shows up and lays nearby, always ready to encourage me with his body language if I am heading in the right direction. It might look quiet to other people, but if you know him well, you know he is actually trying to talk loudly to me, if I will listen! In contrast, my neighbor's dog is not so subtle. Fifteen minutes before dinnertime, she sits in front of you and stares. You can feel her eyes boring a hole through you, and it's very difficult to ignore. Not a perfect analogy, but there are similarities between Cody's communication style and the Holy Spirit's.

The Holy Spirit is always with you, but you can ignore Him. He doesn't speak audibly. He's not loud or pushy—you have to look for Him and pay attention. Everything about His posture says, "over here," "come this way," and He will take the journey *with* you, one step at a time. He is constantly tuned into you, aware of what's going on with you, eagerly anticipating your turning to Him for direction. He will wait while you go off on a tangent but is always ready to point you in the right direction when you ask. He's always ready to show you the next step—and usually *only* the next step. Darn!

One caveat here is that this analogy is more about the Holy Spirit giving guidance or direction, *not* conviction of sin. That would look different. Continuing with the Cody analogy, that's as if you are heading toward sin not expecting to see him, but you look up and, *Boom!* There Cody is. He's peering *at or past* you instead of joining in the way you are headed. He doesn't block your path, and, again, nothing is audible, but He's pointing behind you with his body language saying, "wrong way, go back." That's a picture of how the Spirit's conviction of sin differs from guidance.

Do you struggle to recognize the Spirit's still small voice? What is our role in connecting with Him? What does the Spirit guiding you look like? Can you recognize how He has quietly guided you in situations? If you quiet yourself, is there anything He is saying to you right now?

18

Danger, Bambi!

Cody and a deer

Two are better than one, because
they have a good return for their
labor: If either of them falls down,
one can help the other up. But pity
anyone who falls and has no one to
help them up. Also, if two lie down
together, they will keep warm. But
how can one keep warm alone?
Though one may be overpowered,
two can defend themselves. A cord
of three strands is not quickly bro-
ken.

ECCLESIASTES 4:9-12 NIV

C ody regularly flies out our back door to chase deer over the fence like a savage, wild animal, but on our leashed walks around the block he has learned he is not supposed to jump at them. Amazingly, he generally ignores them. Toward the end of our walk one morning, he lagged behind. I turned to look back at him and noticed a single deer on the hill above us. It's unusual to see a deer by himself, so I said to him (yes, I talk to the deer), "Where are all your friends?" I looked around because when you see one deer there are usually more and I wanted to be prepared in case Cody noticed them and decided to start acting protectively. No, I have *not* forgotten flying through the air at the park.

We continued our walk, and a few paces farther, I turned around again to find the deer starting down the hill as if ready to follow us. He was now just a few yards from Cody. I stopped and began shortening the leash in case Cody jumped. As I turned around, the deer stopped.

Finally figuring out we were not alone, Cody jumped and barked—sending the deer running back up the hill.

I noticed the deer was young. The spots were gone but it was still quite small. I'm convinced sometimes the deer think Cody is one of them. He does kind of look like one at a quick glance, don't ya think?

The deer trotted along the top of the hill parallel to us behind the trees and, at the next opening, started to walk down the hill again as if it was going to fall in line with the pack just behind Cody.

I kept walking slowly, intrigued with the situation. I felt torn. Part of me wanted to see a dog and deer calmly sniffing each other, or even playing together, a Bambi sort of moment. Hey, don't laugh at me. I've seen videos. It happens. On the other hand, I didn't want my arm yanked off, or to find myself facedown in the road. Again, I have *not* forgotten falling at the park. I also didn't want to see the deer hurt, so I paused, causing Cody to perk up, jump and growl at the deer now only six feet away. Yeah, probably not gonna get a Bambi moment.

The deer continued to follow us along the top of the hill through two more yards until we reached our house, and Cody chased him off once more as we climbed the driveway.

So, where were the other deer? Why was that one alone? I sensed if Cody could have gotten free, he was in protective, not play mode, and the deer could have gotten hurt. I'm certain that if the deer was with its usual herd someone older and wiser would have silently communicated, "That is *not* one of us. Danger. Run!"

The Bible talks about the importance of community, of gathering together and walking through life with a group of believers, for the same reasons. Living in community with others can keep us from going astray, becoming confused, thinking something is safe for us that is *not*, and from getting hurt. Can you think of examples where being in a community has kept you from harm? Or the opposite, where *not* being in community has made it easier to walk into danger? What comes to mind for me is the wisdom my husband and I have gleaned when asking for advice about major life decisions. I think also about friends ending dating relationships after receiving unsolicited input from other, and those conversations are hard to have which indicates they really care. Are you in community now? If not and you feel led to, you might take a few minutes to ask the Lord for direction in finding a community that works for you.

19

Mine!

And I saw that all toil and all achievement spring from one person's envy of another. This too is meaningless, a chasing after the wind. **ECCLESIASTES 4:4 NIV**

Our friend's dog Chloe (left) in a tug of war

You are still worldly. For since
there is jealousy and quarreling
among you, are you not worldly?
I CORINTHIANS 3:3 NIV

When our friends travel, we often watch their dogs, and here is the cycle we frequently find ourselves laughing at.

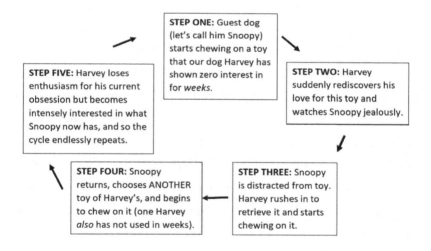

STEP ONE: Guest dog (let's call him Snoopy) starts chewing on a toy that our dog Harvey has shown zero interest in for *weeks*.

STEP TWO: Harvey suddenly rediscovers his love for this toy and watches Snoopy jealously.

STEP THREE: Snoopy is distracted from toy. Harvey rushes in to retrieve it and starts chewing on it.

STEP FOUR: Snoopy returns, chooses ANOTHER toy of Harvey's, and begins to chew on it (one Harvey *also* has not used in weeks).

STEP FIVE: Harvey loses enthusiasm for his current obsession but becomes intensely interested in what Snoopy now has, and so the cycle endlessly repeats.

As human spectators, my husband and I find this quite entertaining, funny, and, as in many of my stories, also sad. Harvey didn't want these old toys until Snoopy used them. These all belonged to Harvey. He could enjoy them at any time, but he didn't. He lost interest—until Snoopy stumbled across them.

While we're talking about how sad this display is, guess what? I confess I did the same thing recently. My husband bought me a pair of Bluetooth wireless headphones to wear while training for a half marathon. I liked them at first but found myself reverting back to my old headphones with the long cord. Sure, the cord was annoying—especially when doing yardwork—but there were positives. The wireless headphones became uncomfortable when worn for extended periods of time, and you had to remember to charge them. They had a strap that stretched around the back of the head which didn't work well when wearing a hat. It was also less intuitive to answer a phone call with the wireless headphones.

I bought my husband the same pair of wireless headphones as a gift. He loved them, wore them all the time: while walking the dog, taking conference calls, and working out. Then one day they broke. He asked about using *mine*. While I *should* have said "You can HAVE mine since I don't use them," instead, I hesitated and eventually let him *borrow* them until the new pair we ordered came in. Why? No good reason. I'm embarrassed to even tell you this story. I'm sure what was going through my head was, "What if *someday* I really need the wireless feature? What if the current pair I am using breaks and I need a backup?" Ask my husband, I'm BIG on having backups. "What if?"

I can be tempted to believe there is not enough, so I hold onto things too tightly and always like to have a backup, or two. I am aware of this, and continually ask God to increase my trust in Him to meet my needs, to be my provider, to be my enough—so that I don't hold onto things too tightly or covet them. Of course, there are many things that I didn't know existed, and I didn't know how much I *needed*—I mean "wanted" them—until I saw someone else with them.

Where do you see yourself in this? Do you struggle with wanting what others have—things you didn't need until you noticed others had them? I have developed strategies to limit my exposure to all the tempting stuff out there. One way is by muting ads on social media. When I have to let an ad play, I turn down the sound and don't pay attention to the product. I'm also not on social media very often. What are some strategies you could employ? How about incorporating reminders in your daily life to refocus your gaze on your loving, heavenly Father who gives *good* gifts, will give you everything you need, and IS everything you need. Ephesians tells us we have been blessed in the heavenly realms with every spiritual blessing in Christ.

20

Pursuing Others

If possible, so far as it depends on you, be at peace with all people.
ROMANS 12:18 NASB

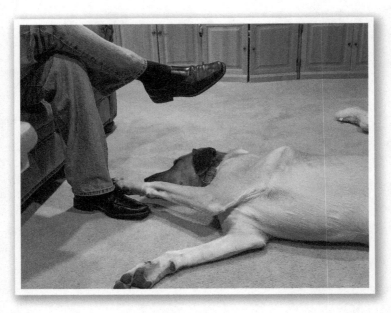

Cody asking for attention

This picture is hilarious. No, really, HILARIOUS. Why is it funny? Because they say dogs are perceptive, pick up on nonverbals, and can read people.

There are five people in this room. Everyone in this room loves dogs—except for one. All of the people in this room will go out of their way to pet a dog, talk to a dog, get down on the dog's level and play with them—except for one. Want to guess which one is not so fond of dogs? Bingo. The one whose attention and affection Cody is seeking.

These are guests from out of town. When they arrived, the dog lovers looked Cody in the eye, said hello to him, and petted him. The other one was fine with him. He doesn't hate dogs, but he didn't make any extra effort—no extra hello, extended eye contact, nothing. When Cody came up to welcome him, he probably moved away to indicate his disinterest. I'm sure in human terms this guy sent rejecting "I'm not interested in you" messages.

And again, whose attention is Cody trying to get? That one who is snubbing him. Cody is loving and accepting someone who is not loving and accepting him back.

I see a lesson in this. Are we good at loving, and even making some sort of *effort* to connect and have a good relationship with all people we come across, or do we only make an effort with the ones who are nice to us?

What pops into my mind as I write this are those people in my life who just don't seem to be happy and come across as rude. Since *I* don't encounter anyone like that on a regular basis, ahem, wink, wink, let's say a restaurant server who just seems determined to scowl and not smile while they work. Sadly, my initial gut reaction too often is to take offense and think, *What's your problem?* On other occasions, though, my well-rested-had-time-with-Jesus-this-morning self shows up, considers that I really don't know what is going on in their world, shouldn't judge, and chooses to intentionally be kind.

A friend of mine and I have been known to start a competition: who can get them to smile first? Often as we strike up a conversation and express interest in the "target," the cold façade fades and they warm up, sometimes even sharing horrible circumstances they are walking through which sheds light on their demeanor, and I feel terrible for taking offense. Yes, sometimes we even get them to smile! And truly, is this not a small picture of what we are to do as Christ's ambassadors? To take interest in and "see" others, to love them—even those that are a bit hard to?

Is there someone in your life who tends to be prickly or is cold with you? Maybe someone who acts downright rejecting toward you? Lord, where could I be more open and make advances toward someone who seems unfriendly to me?

21

Like Owner, Like Dog

Do not be yoked together with unbelievers. For what do righteousness and wickedness have in common? Or what fellowship can light have with darkness?
2 CORINTHIANS 6:14 NIV

Photo by Valerie Elash on Unsplash

*Therefore encourage one another
and build one another up, just as
you are doing.*
1 THESSALONIANS 5:11 ESV

E ver notice how *some* dogs, not all of course, look like their owners and even act like them? For example, I can think of several friends who have a short, stocky build and own English bulldogs. You rarely see strong bodybuilders with fluffy, yappy, little dogs. Likewise, I can think of friends with a tall, wiry physique who own similar looking dogs.

I found it an entertaining exercise to think through my friends and their dogs and see how many fit this concept. It doesn't fit all, but some were oddly similar. I understand the argument that we tend to choose dogs that are like us, and I agree with that. We, for example, intentionally choose calm, laid back dogs as that fits our lifestyle.

So, what about personality? Does it follow the same pattern? Think through your friends and their dogs' temperaments. Are they similar? Sure, some of that is breed but there is also an argument for environment.

Our current dog, Cody, was a rescue. As mentioned before, we are rescue attempt number two for him. His foster parents indicated they did not know what happened at his first forever home, but he returned to them a different dog. He wouldn't go in a crate, or he'd break out. He was anxious and would pace and whine. His temperament had changed.

It took a few months, but after coming to us he did calm down. No more waking us up pacing and whining at 4 am—*thank goodness!* Eventually, he became comfortable lying in his crate again. His whole demeanor calmed down. Part of that was getting used to his new environment, but not all of it, as his previous home obviously didn't "instill the chill." When people first meet Cody, they often comment on how calm he is. We laugh and give each other a knowing look, thinking, *Sometimes. You haven't seen him in action chasing planes!*

Some of his change in behavior is a result of his new environment and the people he is around—and who he is not around. My husband and I are definitely not high energy, loud, extroverted personalities. Our home is a calm place, and Cody has reflected that and become calmer.

Numerous studies show we influence each other. We become like those we spend time with. This is one reason the Bible tells us not to be yoked to unbelievers, as well as to not forsake meeting together with the saints.

Have a little fun and take a minute to think about your friends and their dogs. Do they have similar personalities? Looking beyond the breed's temperament, can you see the influence of the dogs' environments on their personalities? If you are an owner, what does your dog's personality say about your home's atmosphere? Consider taking a minute and asking the Lord if there are changes that He would have you make in terms of who you spend time with and who influences you, as well as where you are an influence on others. Is there an atmosphere in your home He is revealing to you that is not healthy? What is a first step you could take to change it? In my life that usually looks like acknowledging it, confessing it, and asking Him to fill that space.

Photo by Mattheus Bertelli on Pexels

22

Unhealed Places

It is better to live in a corner of the housetop than in a house shared with a quarrelsome wife.

PROVERBS 21:9 ESV

Sammie

Better is open rebuke than hidden love. Wounds from a friend can be trusted ...

PROVERBS 27:5-6 NIV

While visiting Ohio, I walked with my sister, Paula, and her dog Sammie (a rescued Cockapoo, Cocker Spaniel, and Poodle mix). He was very sweet with people but *not* good with other dogs. I'm sorry. I don't think I communicated that clearly. He was *awful, terrible, a hot mess* with other dogs. He was all of twenty-five pounds, and when another dog passed, he transformed from calm, happy, and cute to possessed, crazed, and foaming at the mouth. I found it disruptive and stressful. My sister and I couldn't have a conversation. I couldn't complete a thought without a Sammie meltdown—maybe a slight exaggeration. We were constantly on the lookout for other dogs so we could alter our path to avoid them.

After the walk, we went for lunch and sat outside with the same constant interruptions. Sammie transitioned from Dr. Jekyll to Mr. Hyde whenever another dog walked by, and he was uncontrollable. The conversation revolved around, "Watch out, here comes another dog," instead of updates on our lives. While we spent several hours together, I didn't connect with my sister in a meaningful way.

As with most rescues, we don't know the full story of Sammie's background. My sister indicated she was working on training. I assume Sammie either never had training, so he thought he was alpha and shielding us from danger, or, due to previous bad encounters with dogs, was afraid—and protecting himself and us from danger. Meltdowns were Sammie in protection mode. Poor Sammie! He had never worked through his issues, and he really was such a sweet dog.

I want to give Sammie grace, but if I could communicate something to precious little Sammie and others, a few acquaintances maybe, it's this: "I love you, but your unhealed places make you NO FUN to be around. No, I'm not kidding Sammie. I do *not* want to go on another walk with you and Paula again. Paula sure, but I would hope she leaves you at home. Or can I have a guarantee we will not pass other dogs? Just wanted to lovingly tell you that. Any chance you could seek some healing and counseling my friend? I'd like to *want* to walk with you sometime, but right now, I just dread it."

But we don't say that kind of thing to each other. What do we do? With unpleasant people, we distance ourselves and avoid them. When they are included, our calendar is suddenly full, or we stay far away. Here's the thing, though. It's often easier for others to see our unhealed places than for us to recognize them.

I don't want to be that way. When seeing others' unpleasant behavior which makes me want to put distance in the relationship, I try to be intentional about praying for them, for their healing in that area. Do I walk this perfectly? Of course not! But I sure hope others would do that for *me* rather than just judge me and withdraw. I also try to remember to ask myself if I do the *same* behaviors —and too often the answer is yes.

If you don't think you have any unhealed places, consider humbly asking your closest friends. Be prepared to listen without responding. It's challenging to give this kind of feedback. Be thankful if your friends are willing to be honest with you about this. If you don't have close friends who would give you this kind of feedback, could this issue be part of the reason? Pray that God would lead you to a safe group or counselor.

Bottom line, our unhealed places make us no fun to be around. Think about someone this reminds you of. How does it feel to be around them when they are in the middle of that unpleasant behavior? Yuck, right? I don't want to cause others to feel that way. So, let's ask God to expose these places in us and choose to walk into them with Him for healing. Lord, where does this impact me, my life? Show me the next unhealed place you would like to address. I commit to press into You for your healing. I trust you are GOOD, and I want to be enjoyable to be around.

Sammie and Paula

23

Let Your Yes Be Yes

*If a man vows a vow to the Lord
... he shall not break his word. He
shall do according to all that pro-
ceeds out of his mouth.*
NUMBERS 30:2 ESV

Aslan ready for a road trip

Let what you say be simply 'Yes'
or 'No'; anything more than this
comes from evil.
MATTHEW 5:37 ESV

As I mentioned in the introduction, my dad grew up in a time when dogs were work animals and never allowed indoors. They certainly were not an integral part of the family. One Thanksgiving we missed making kennel reservations and inquired about bringing our Mastiff, Aslan, with us to visit my parents. Knowing Dad's position on dogs, I asked if he would let us bring Aslan in just at night and close him up in the kitchen.

I hoped this might be a good compromise. Though Aslan was a dog and not human, we *did* consider him a part of *our* family unit, and dogs *do* have feelings. He had never been left outside all night and wasn't accustomed to Cleveland's frigid weather. It was going to be hard enough on him being tied up outside or in the car while we were at my parents' house, and it would only be one night. Respecting my dad's authority to make the rules for his house, I wanted to be clear about handling this situation ahead of time.

Well, he said yes, but here's how I suspect that looked. I asked my mom, who went and asked my dad. He sighed, mumbled underneath his breath, grumbled about it, and then begrudgingly said, "Well, I *guess* so." Meaning, he didn't want to but said yes anyway. I knew he wasn't going to be excited about it, but he said yes.

Aslan made the holiday rounds with us that year. At my parents' house, I waited as long as possible to bring him inside that night suspecting my dad wasn't thrilled about the situation. As I settled Aslan in for the night and closed the kitchen doors, Dad started grumbling and complaining. He didn't go as far as telling me to put Aslan back out, but in his own way he made it loud and clear he did not want Aslan inside. So, what was I to do? All kennels were full at the holidays, plus it was after hours. I was nine hours from home, one hour from my in-laws, and it was November in Cleveland, Ohio, so it was cold!

Of course, I was ticked off. It was more about the principle of it all than anything else. I asked. He said yes. *What's the deal, Dad? Don't play games with me **now**.* This may seem like a silly little example with minor consequences, but what were those consequences? I was hurt and mad at my dad. It's been a while now, so the details are fuzzy, but I'm sure I did not communicate lovingly and respectfully at the time. I was stressed. It caused tension and strife in our relationship. It sure didn't help build my trust in Dad.

He did not let his "yes be yes" and his "no be no" and basically went back on his word. Also, he was playing games, right? He really didn't say no. He just went about his way, whining, complaining, and attempting to make me feel guilty so he would not *have* to say "no." I had a good track record for giving in and doing what he wanted since I am usually a rule follower, peacekeeper, and people pleaser.

Looking back at this many years later and having less tolerance for mind games, isn't that all just icky? Games like that can mess up our relationships. It ruins our testimony. It really turns me off, but I bet if you asked my husband, he could provide examples in my own life where I have done the same thing. Maybe I don't want to let someone down, so I make excuses to avoid saying no.

I try not to promise things I cannot do, but I'm sure there are instances where I have knowingly overpromised to make someone happy in person, only to back out by e-mail later. I *also* procrastinate, hoping a good excuse comes up, instead of saying no to something I don't want to do. Is this just me? Am I the only one who is not honest in all my communication? I suspect not. Take a minute and ask the Father if there are places where you could improve your communication. Ask Him what drives you to be less than honest and direct with others. Yes, there is a point that you don't always have to say *exactly* what you are thinking or be blunt. How you say things matters, but our communication should still be honest.

24

Dogs Eat Each Other's SH--T!

Not poop, but Cody just threw up and is about to consume his own, well, you know. Gross!

We demolish arguments and
every pretension that sets itself up
against the knowledge of God, and
we take captive every thought to
make it obedient to Christ.

2 CORINTHIANS 10:5 NIV

Dogs eat other dog's sh-t!! I worried while writing this that the title may be a little too vulgar and turn people off but decided to stick with it. If my language is a bit harsh or shocking, I'm okay with that. I'm glad I've gotten your attention because this is serious.

Dogs eat other dog's sh-t!! What is that about? Let's think about this. It's another dog's waste. It has questionable nutritional value. It's dirty. Sometimes it has worms. It reeks and it's repulsive. It's GROSS! Take a moment and consider that awful stench—and they actually *eat* it—like, take it in and let it slowly work its way through their system. Okay, I'm about to throw up now it's so disgusting. Are you? Good, because guess what? We do the same thing. Oh yes. We do, too!

So maybe it's not *exactly* the same but consider this. We take the ugly words people say or infer about us and accept them. We let them affect us. We take them in, own them, and let the ideas become part of our psyche. It's the same as crap. It has no beneficial value. It stinks. It's repulsive. Yet some of this stuff we hear or is directed our way isn't even really about us. It's coming from something going on in the other person. They are hurting or in a bad place, and since misery loves company, or it makes the person feel good at the moment, they lash out at us. And we, for lack of a better analogy, "eat" their words and take them in. We let them influence us even though it's harmful, not true, and *crap*!

Let me give a few personal examples. One night my dad tried to teach me math. Out of his frustration and irritation with my failure to grasp whatever he was trying to teach, he yelled, "Are you an idiot? Are you an imbecile?" I still remember this, and it is only with time that I realized the situation may have reflected more his lack of ability to be patient and teach than my ability to grasp that material.

Then there was the time I heard two guys in front of me in the ski lift line say, "She'd be pretty except for her nose." I don't walk around insecure about my nose, but I sure do carry the sense of not being pretty or good enough at times. Or the kids who laughed at me and said, "You're a re-re-re-retard!" I used to stutter severely. Alone with just myself and Jesus, I am confident of my value and worth. Put other people in the room, though, and I start to expect the familiar criticism and rejection that they may not even be thinking but someone said a long time ago, and which was, let's just say, crap!. But I "ate" it. I took it in and let it settle deep in my gut rather than letting it bounce off or ignoring it, and I can still be tempted to believe it.

I'm confident you've experienced the same. What destructive lies or ideas that others have said or implied about you have you accepted as truth and let become a part of your ethos? These agreements can be hard to identify. They are familiar and sort of just hang out as the backdrop of your life—so be patient and persistent in seeking them out. Ask God to reveal them to you and then do like Jeremiah talks about and replace them with truth by "eating" God's word and letting it bring you freedom and joy as it integrates into your system instead of the crap! This is huge people, incredibly freeing, and worth the time spent.

25

Who Me? Naaa, It Was the Dog!

One who conceals his wrongdoings will not prosper, But one who confesses and abandons them will find compassion.
PROVERBS 28:13 NASB

Who, me?

I'm not going to say we've all *"done"* it, but I think we've all experienced this—dog owners, that is. You're relaxing with friends or family, including the family dog—let's call him Snoopy—and suddenly, a familiar stench wafts across your nostrils.

As people catch a whiff of this they start looking around in search of the source—in order to shame them of course. People look back and forth trying to find the culprit. Someone launches an accusation, "Ahh <fill in the name>, eewww!" But who *also* always gets blamed—most likely by the guilty party? Snoopy. "Ugh! Snoopy! Why did you do that?"

I have a large dog, and over half of the time I think he really *is* to blame—and boy, can he clear out a room. Still, he's not to blame *all* the time. So, what's up with this avoidance? Why do we do this? We haven't moved beyond the original story of blame shifting like in the Garden of Eden. And over something so universal. Not that I would know, ahem.

I find this a comical reminder of how we immediately, instinctively, lean toward covering up, hiding, and blaming others. Trivial though it may be, it is an illustration of how the proverbial apple has not fallen far from the tree. I'm sure if we sipped coffee together you could share examples with more serious consequences.

Thank goodness I don't have to hide my bad behavior from Jesus. He knows it all anyway, *and* He knows my motives. Yet, He still loves me—though not necessarily my stench behavior. I feel relieved, knowing I don't have to hide.

As you sit quietly and seek Him, ask Him if there are any places you are hiding or blame shifting—that are more serious than passing gas. If something comes to mind, are you willing to confess it as sin? Ask Him to cultivate your ability to both accept and own how deeply He loves you, so that you can avoid falling for the temptation to blame others for your behavior.

26

Live Like Someone Left the Gate Open

You make known to me the path of life; in your presence there is fullness of joy; at your right hand are pleasures forevermore.

PSALM 16:11 ESV

Photo by Arjan Stalpers on Unsplash

L ive like someone left the gate open. Recently, I've been seeing this saying in gift stores. It's usually on wall plaques or decorative towels and has a picture of a dog running at full gallop with a gleeful, happy smile (yes, my friend Wiebke tells me dogs do "smile"). Oh my gosh, I just love that saying. It speaks to me. It captures something I think we all yearn for.

We don't have the space for our dog, Cody, to let loose and all out run, so when he has a chance to be totally free, it's spectacular to watch. He's had a few chances to run off leash at the beach, and once he realizes he is not restrained, he takes off like someone testing the limits of a new sports car. His first laps around us are fast but also jubilant and playful. He comes back with this happy, satisfied look as if he's saying, "THAT is what these legs were made for!"

And, I don't have to imagine what it would look like if I left the gate open because, um, I have (yikes! Sorry Joe). On one such occasion I was in the woods behind our home explaining to the neighbors that Cody was tall and fawn color, and kind of looked like a deer. Immediately the son pointed behind me and said, "Like that?" And I watched six deer run by with Cody hot on their heels. He didn't slow down at all but glanced sideways at me as he sailed by with a gleeful look that I interpreted as "Hi! OMG! This is SO MUCH FUN!"

As I think about what is so attractive about this phrase to me, I return to what I wrote earlier about dogs and unconditional love. They don't live in their heads or play mind games. They just live. There's something in that freedom and joyful play which I can learn from and want to grow into. Maybe you can, too. As children of the King, our chains are broken but sometimes our lives don't reflect this. What would it look like for you to pursue joy, to run your race uninhibited, to live each day with that kind of freedom? Do you need to be reminded the gate IS open, now? I do! Let Him speak to your heart on this.

Cody and a new friend running free on the beach

27

"Keep Hope Alive"

*May the God of hope fill you with
all joy and peace in believing, so
that by the power of the Holy spirit
you may abound in hope.*
ROMANS 15:13 ESV

Cody hoping for a car trip that is not in the current plan

H ope is such an important ... thing? Funny, as I write that I wonder, what is hope? Is it a concept? Is it a feeling? We don't talk about *feeling* hope much. We talk about *having* hope. I guess we do talk about feeling hopeful. Maybe this is foreign to me because I don't live in hope much? Hmmm.

I know hope is critically important. Depression can be defined as the lack of hope. It is said that suicidal people have "lost their hope." The way we talk about hope I find interesting. We can have it. We can lose it. I hear the idea of *choosing* joy often. Can we also choose hope? Maybe hope is the result of faith which some define as choosing to believe in that which we cannot see.

What does hope look like? As I think about this, I hear an expression my husband frequently utters, "Keep hope alive." This phrase has been used with all our dogs. Joe will say this when we are eating or preparing dinner and our dogs appear, positioning themselves in front of the food, staring at it intently. "Keep hope alive, Cody. Keep hope alive." They usually end up getting a bite, so maybe it's not the best example of hope!

Here's another one. If you are a dog owner, ever notice how getting up and walking around signals opportunity? For example, when we walk by the laundry room, or put tennis shoes on, or go to the garage to put the recyclables in the bin, these patterns hint a "pack adventure" of some kind may be in store, and our dogs perk their ears up, suddenly tuned in with a gleam in their eye. Is that not a great picture of hope? The majority of the time these behaviors do not lead to anything exciting. I really am *just* getting the mail or putting the laundry in the dryer. Even so, the next time, there they are, standing by the door, still hoping for fun and excitement.

This reminds me of our Mastiff, Aslan. I started to realize he could tell when I was ending a phone call even before I did. If he was lying nearby, he would get up and stand there staring at me with a "Yay! Come play with me. Throw the ball," look in his eye. He knew transition times were chances to influence me to play.

Here's a third picture of hope. When I unload groceries and put them away, this is never a time Cody gets food. Cody might get a scrap of our food at the end of a meal, and treats at other times, but *never* when I unload groceries. Yet, as I carry them inside, he consistently comes and greets me, eagerly watching as I unload items and put them in the fridge, hoping for a treat. This might be another time Joe would say, "Keep hope alive, Cody. Keep hope alive," meaning you never get anything but here you are always hoping that a good thing is coming your way.

Of course Cody doesn't understand this, but a human could recognize that this food being unpacked is eventually going to be turned into a meal of which he may get a scrap. Isn't that a bit of a picture of what the Bible means when it talks about hope being in things yet to come? We don't have them now but believe they are destined in our future?

What does hope look like to you, that eager anticipation of something good to come? Remember that snapshot in your mind. Is there a place in your life where you could use hope? Try inserting the feeling produced by that image. How does that feel? Can you sense hope growing? Do you find yourself resisting? What holds you back? Take some time right now and talk to Jesus about that.

This is Cody "hoping" for an outing. This look says, "Hmmm ... you're putting on tennis shoes. Are you taking out the trash or are we taking a walk. Or...?"

28

Loyalty

Madison, the loyal one.
Photo courtesy of Shayla Sullivan.

The Lord himself goes before you
and will be with you; he will
never leave you nor forsake you.
DEUTERONOMY 31:8a NIV

A story from the dreadful California wildfires of 2018 first caught my attention because it was about an Anatolian Shepherd mix, which is what we thought our dog Cody was, and you don't hear about that breed often. It is an inspiring story I will never forget because of the beautiful picture of loyalty.

There are many tales from those fires where the families had to evacuate quickly, and the livestock guardian dog refused to leave. One Great Pyrenees protected the family's goats with fire encroaching on all sides, and even picked up a group of deer as well. In most of these cases, the family was allowed back the next day, or soon afterwards.

The story of this Anatolian, Madison, amazes me because the owners weren't able to return for an entire month. An animal rescue worker did check on Madison and left her food and water. Four weeks later, the family came home and found their faithful dog lying by the driveway protecting the property—and by property I literally mean "land" because everything else burned down. There was no house, just a blackened landscape, but there was Madison.

Is that not a beautiful picture of dependability and loyalty? There, *one month* later, Madison was still at her post defending charred ruins. Is that not also in part why we view dogs as having unconditional love? They, at least this breed, stay; they protect, even when times get tough. I like to think of myself as dependable because I try to honor my word and do what I say I'm going to, follow through on commitments, and not be wishy washy, but I don't feel loyal when I think about Madison!

May this story of one dog's loyalty remind us about our Heavenly Father. He stays. He protects. He's always on guard. He doesn't get scared, or lonely, or hungry, or leave His post. If we get hurt or mad at Him and stop talking to Him for a while, He's always right there when we get back—He hasn't moved. Let's just take a moment to consider these marvelous attributes and thank Him.

Madison on her property. Photo courtesy of Shayla Sullivan.

29

First Responder

Cody on the edge of barking at thunder

Do nothing from selfish ambition or conceit, but in humility count others more significant than your-selves. PHILIPPIANS 2:3 ESV

... for God gave us a spirit not of fear but of power and love and self-control. 2 TIMOTHY 1:7 ESV

One of our dog Cody's nicknames is "First Responder" because he amazingly has the instinct to run *toward* danger rather than away from it.

While we were walking him one day in July, we heard fireworks nearby. He growled, looked for the cause of the noise, and wanted to pull us in that direction with a "let me at it" stance.

This grabbed our attention because our previous dogs had a very different reaction to danger. Our dog Harvey would look for cover or a corner and lie there shaking and panting, poor thing, and while people thought our 195-pound Mastiff would be tough and protect us, I'm not so sure. During walks when a neighbor's chocolate lab, Belushi, came out and barked, Aslan would get BEHIND us and bark back!

Cody is quite different. At the dog park, he is often a bit aloof, prefer-ring to walk the perimeter and pick up on local gossip, smelling the news, instead of playing. However, when other dogs start to get too rowdy and on the edge of a fight, Cody comes running in like a cop or a bouncer. I like to interpret his body language as, "What's going on here? Break it up," as He calmly walks into the middle of the action unintimidated.

His behavior also stands out because it is so foreign to me. I wish I was more like Cody. I am writing this during the fear and panic of the Coronavirus pandemic. When I sense danger, my initial instinct is to run and hide, to protect myself, stock up on supplies, and think of my own self-preservation instead of others' well-being. I *wish* my first, automatic response was to rush in and fight danger, to be willing to put myself in harm's way to help others. I'm not kidding when I say I'm jealous. I really want to be that kind of person and I struggle with hating and judging myself for not being hardwired that way.

So, my personal challenge is to accept myself the way God made me, recognize my programming and tendency to react in fear, and take steps to counteract it. I have reminders to continually set my gaze on God and not my circumstances. I intentionally choose what I listen to (including not constantly listening to 24-hour news media about the Coronavirus right now, for example). Some days I carry scriptures on index cards and refer to them frequently.

There is a song out right now, "Reckless Love" by Cory Asbury, that my husband has nicknamed, "Jesus is a Navy Seal." You know, the one about Jesus kicking down walls and climbing up mountains to come after me.

I think Jesus is a first responder, too. He went—and still goes—into battle for us. He willingly served and sacrificed for our benefit. His Spirit shields us from evil today. I'm so thankful for that. I'm so glad for the battle He has already won. I'm so grateful He continues to fight for us. May I continue to find my strength in Him.

What about you? Are you a first responder personality bravely walking into danger to protect others, or are you like me? I would be the dog cowering under the table when trouble arises, I suspect. If you, like me, struggle with fear, take a moment and invite God to speak to your heart about His protection, His trustworthiness. Ask Him to grow in you the ability to trust Him day to day and not live in fear, to be aware of the needs of others, and to be willing to serve.

Magnificence of God's Creation

*O Lord, how manifold are your
works! In wisdom you have made
them all; the earth is full of your
creatures. Here is the sea, great
and wide, which teems with creatures innumerable, living things
both small and great.*
PSALM 104:24-25 ESV

*Cody in attack mode protecting us from a horseshoe crab, then later in
submissive mode asking us to rub his belly*

E ver have random moments that remind you how awe-inspiring God's creation is? Here's one of mine. My dog Cody thinks he can protect us from lightning, planes, and fireworks—silly boy. While we are "under siege," he growls and runs all over the house barking at the "threat." This can be amusing—but also annoying and disruptive when we are trying to watch TV or entertain guests. Upon first meeting him, people frequently comment on how calm and gentle Cody is. I laugh to myself thinking, "Sometimes, but you might be surprised if you saw him in action, growling ferociously with a snarl on his face— intimidating, to say the least."

He reminds me of a lion when he is in protective mode. As I think about it, he does have the coloring of a lion, and the general body shape and large feet of one. He stalks animals and saunters with a gait similar to a lion. Though he is only 130 pounds, he is tall, and when I sit next to him on the floor, he seems *huge*. If he was not friendly and decided to attack or eat me, he would totally win! Again, intimidating!

Cody can also be sweet and gentle. He gives soft kisses on my face to say hello when I come home then runs into the other room to chew his bone. When he wants me to pet him, he nudges my arm or just stands and stares. I've forgotten to feed him because he doesn't aggressively beg but comes to lie near me and patiently waits.

So, here is this amazing creature living in my home, one minute acting like a savage, wild animal—protecting me, I think. How cool is that? Until you realize it is from an airplane! Then, only moments later once the threat has passed, Cody comes over, lays at my feet, and rests a paw on my leg asking, "Rub my belly?" Although he is independent and would take charge if given the chance, we have established ourselves as alphas, so he listens to and obeys us.

There is something here that I feel at a loss to articulate well. It is magnificent and beautiful that this potentially wild creature which acts vicious at times will also sit and stay when I tell him to and seek my affection.

Have you been surprised by the beauty and majesty of God's creation recently? When? Where? Have you seen it in any of your animals or pets? If not, pay attention. Ask God to reveal Himself, then watch for your random moment of revelation. It will look and sound completely different than mine. Finally, let the impact of just how phenomenal God's creation is wash over you.

Enjoy the stories?

Honest reviews help an author more than any marketing campaign. Please rate the book online. It doesn't matter if you thought it was a mediocre 3-star or a fantastic 5. The number of reviews matters more than the rating. Thank you.

Also By Christine

Upcoming works by Christine include another month of doggie devotionals, plus a month dedicated to God's truths revealed in nature. Stay in touch for updates.

https://www.facebook.com/aCoupleOfWriters

Made in the USA
Monee, IL
22 December 2024

75232987R00075